The house is still standing

The house is still standing

ADRIENNE BARRETT

icehouse poetry
an imprint of Goose Lane Editions

Edited by Katia Grubisic.
Cover and interior images detailed from "Bwthyn glan môr" © 2010 by Valériane Leblond, valeriane-leblond.eu
Cover and page design by Julie Scriver.
Printed in Canada.
10 9 8 7 6 5 4 3 2 1

Library and Archives Canada Cataloguing in Publication

Barrett, Adrienne, 1972-
    The house is still standing / Adrienne Barrett.

Poems.

ISBN 978-0-86492-904-4

    I. Title.
PS8603.A738H69 2013      C811'.6      C2012-907159-5


Goose Lane Editions acknowledges the generous support of the Canada Council for the Arts, the Government of Canada through the Canada Book Fund (CBF), and the Government of New Brunswick through the Department of Tourism, Heritage, and Culture.

Goose Lane Editions
500 Beaverbrook Court, Suite 330
Fredericton, New Brunswick
CANADA E3B 5X4
www.gooselane.com

*When I was a little child I used to pray, fervently, fearfully, that when I should be grown up I might never forget what I thought and felt and suffered then.*

—E. Nesbit

*We have not journeyed across the centuries, across the oceans, across the mountains, across the prairies, because we are made of sugar candy.*

—Winston Churchill

# Contents

## One

## Two

## Three

*One*

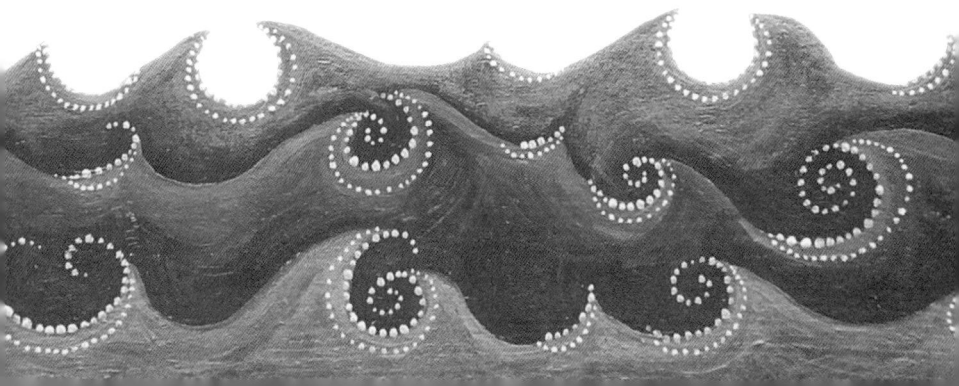

## Construction

I was high on the scaffolding. It was springtime. Far above the wall I'd made, I stood upon a narrow plank of splitting wood; wood barely overlapping its steel arms, braces barely holding. When I moved, it moved. So high it hurt at highest pitch. I stilled myself, the only thing not still the blood singing through the circuitry. Someone clambered up to rescue me.

The window casts itself on the opposite wall. Black macramé of branches; arts and crafts for witches born under Cancer. Homebodies and wallflowers.

I dreamed I was high on the scaffolding. So dark in the warehouse, the din and heat and a pickaxe sighing against rock. Welders' torches flashed. Men dismantled boards and braces on every side, leaving mine for last. I became an island and a tower, the breath knocked out of me. Hours I knit myself together, awaited rescue. I might be waiting still.

The trees stand in rows, and down the black coral branches runs a squirrel. From branch to branch it springs, down and down.

## The ferocious list-maker, as children

Sunsets got me high while people
scratched their armpits. My third day of first grade,
I was bumped to second. On the fifth day, third.
I was surprised it stopped there;
I thought I'd keep climbing forever. I ate
language, inhaled friends, ran three-legged races
with God. To write a list
was rapture.

My soft-skinned mother didn't do much
in the way of mothering. My father died
on business; months later,
somebody bothered
to tell me. My stepfather gave
my name, demanded
I say please, thank you, oh yes
a very nice time.

Time! I had to conquer each poet,
piece of music, scientific paradigm;
to be worthy. Lust,
love demanded my scalpel. No use
for niceties, nor for irony. Everything
mattered. Though I fought it tooth
and nail, I stayed a child.

# Transubstantiation

Finicky business, breastfeeding
hardcover in hand.
Though rocking-chair
page turns are nothing
compared with my wriggles
to wheedle the jeans down
around my knees
while I hold a screaming baby; I pee,
wipe, tug them back up
inch by inch,
left hip, right hip;
jam paper-cracked hands
somehow under a somehow
running faucet, bubble and squeak.
(The baby's screaming, remember.)

The novel is innocuous. I wonder several times
why it's won awards. We're just noodling along,
the book and I, in what I think
is symbiosis (I get a nice story, the book
gets to be read)

when the narrator's
mother—steamer trunk
of a woman—is hacked
into pieces with a machete and
fed to the pigs.

Breasts full, squirting
madly. He's cradled against me,
trusting, hungry,
warm little swallows
audible to his father across the room
who is watching the game
in the half-light.

## Little Hiroshima

It was dark night
my mom was puking
thin liquid yellow thin as water
quiet the lady in the next bed lay
she wasn't eating only wasting
away my mom was weeping the light
of the bathroom was harsh
white the gown
fell open
she sat
on the toilet
as the gown came down
around her bandages
with dried blood where
what only this morning
would fill your hand
wasn't there anymore     a little
Hiroshima it has been called     my mother's
hair is soft and brown her skin
is warm and white-brown she looks
like a little girl without
her glasses we told her
as we trotted alongside the gurney
as she was wheeled down the hall
towards surgery
she smiled said really
we kissed her
waited
in her hospital room where her friend
who had experience with such things

told me not
to sit on the bed
because I crawled
with contaminants
my
mom is sobbing on the toilet my mom naked
and cold the nurse will not come there is only one
small towel already soaked on the tile floor.

## As the ice storm flags

Murky skin of a canned plum,
the sea. Six horses in a field, startled

into stillness. White globes cling
to the windshield. Dusty sheen

of a pool slide remembers flesh, heart
steers itself out of my bundled chest.

Only a week before, this road
shot through gold-suffused air.

Now a blackbird flaps its wings and
time is slow.

I have never cared for birds. Sky,
what else have you got?

# The kaleidoscope, as children

Many collections, and each
was a world. I gazed at my
leaflets without reading
a word. They shone
and were symmetrical.

I kept a tub of lady
birds who clamoured
in the hundreds. Mr. Thraves
set them free for reasons
now clear to me, though
at the time I was hysterical.

Silence gleamed like silver. Silence ran
down a windowpane;
but I didn't have a name
for the hurt that
hurt me.

I went to the woods
because leaves fall
in spirals; sat among coins
stacked into towers;
examined the spine
of each book at the library. Later
I learned that the word was lonely.

At nighttime, I walked
a landscape of numbers.
Days, I ran barefoot,
clutching socks full
of conkers.

# Suspension

My body and I, we're
        not strung
to anyone. Sometimes
        we tug upon
a tampon, or clutch
        another sort
of rope that dangles
        seemingly
from heaven; it's almost
        as though on occasion
God heeds the bell pull
        stoops
to pluck us by the cords
        that wrap us like a round
of beef;
        and we're carried, buoyant
from today to tomorrow
        at startlingly little expense
to ourselves. But
        mostly we run loose
we two. No one
        intrudes,
alters, soothes.

# Madonna with three childless writers

No flinching when the subject arises.
It isn't for lack of wanting, more
a matter of circumstance. One of you
has black leaves for eyes. The second
once had a stepdaughter who came,
then went. And the last, like tumbling water,
you've mothered brothers
and sisters. You've mothered.

Guilt, like a rich woman. Wolfing
down the tapas, nouveau
riche. This afternoon's housefly
in an overturned glass,
released at dusk
to pasture on these vast
bistro plates, giddy to slurp
the beefy, marbled conversations
that once were Sunday dinner. Friends,

under your gaze I'm conscious
that my days
are so everyday. You hand me
questions that weigh a stone;
I throw pebbles at them. But there's comfort
where my belly swells. I grant
it's a flutter
to be seen as exotic,

a cow among gazelles.
My little girl, I tell you three
madonnas with empty laps,
didn't seem quite real

until the day I woke her
from a nap, licked her tears
and found they tasted different
from my own. I'm aware of being
precious, of wanting to be taken
for your kind, as the furnace
that moves your words across the page
hums in my ear.
All the same, she tasted strange.

## The fearless hyena, as children

They called me Pao-pao.
Cannonball. Twelve pounds
at birth, twelve months
in mom's belly. So they said.

I failed to impress dad.
He had me hoisting sandbags
by the age of four. At heart
I was still lazy, but my muscles learned
where my brain could not. School
was one long drone

and not in a good way.
My body
fell from its chair to land sound
on its rump.
I'd rigged it well. I gave it. Mumbo-jumbo…
splat! The crowds roared for more
so I gave it.

> Sweet bun in my mouth, I rode the ferry
> to the drama academy.
> Dad signed the papers:
> ten years.
> The first weeks
> I gloried in aerial backflips,
> flattery and desserts. Master liked
> to see us smug
> before pulling the rug out from under us.

*You may discipline the boy,*
*even to death.* It was in the contract.
I gobbled one too many candies,
and Master gave me the welts to prove it. After that,
I starved
with the rest of them.

## Terrarium

Little brother is a fighter. This means
sometimes to lose. To watch the loop
of tape, to learn the truth of loss, and this
on top of his everywhere bruises. There he is,
trapped in glass; that's his sacred head
and it's knocking one side to the other. Bells ring
and that's not him anymore.

Then there's my sister, who couldn't
be more transparent. Tap the window; try
to rouse the lizard
lounging in her throat.
When her words flick out, the reptile sometimes
takes the blame. A fantastic scapegoat
though he tickles.
                    Enough. I pulled her aside, said
Sweetheart, what's this sickly impulse
to replace your own flesh
with small squares of glass? Soon
you'll disappear. Admittedly, your ribs are perfect
shelves for buttons, plates, the pine cone
hedgehogs you've made. And
with what single-mindedness
you've sorted the archives—here, the stories
you've been collecting; there, every past mistake. Of course,
any curator makes her errors
as she goes: mixed-up labels, omissions
of provenance. But these can be remedied
tomorrow, you'll see to that.

Just, you always forget
to keep something for yourself.

# What we make from what we've found

Now, Aboyne is the name
    for one of these once-towns
dotting the way

    to our father's house. The ritual
as we drive past the sign: *Aboyne*
    *aboyne aboyne* springing

around on our bums
    though we aren't kids any more
(eight thighs without curves

    snug as crayons
in the back seat,
    two middle sisters

held in place with old-fashioned
    belts from the scrapyard).
It's nice to be a little fatter

    for the cake that gets you there,
for, a sister says, the mad pash;
    but above all these, for buoyancy,

for floating in the lake.
    The small lake feeds a larger.
The millionaire's cottage sits

at the mouth. Beavers dam it
every year. Our father chased
  our mother round

the cloakroom; the kiss
  came ten years later,
lake swimming on a Sunday.

  Our teeth didn't clunk
(her version, meaning
    ecstasy). On the honeymoon

our father tucked his chin,
    wrung the strings
like Jascha Heifetz.

  Our mother hid her head,
had never heard such music.
  Unexpectedly warming,

this extra flesh, bringing me
  closer to her shape
so she's my dwelling place

  again. Sculling underwater
for hours in the shallows
    among the lily pad stems,

red and tangled. Navigating
  fields of conductor wire.
Thick cables of them

hung from our cellar ceiling,
cast-offs from the Company.
    We turned them into braided bracelets,

Christmas trinkets, twist ties
    for the milk bags
that our mother scissored open,

    washed, dried
and filled with liverwurst sandwiches.
    He worked hard, our father,

works hard still
    to play well, sing well, calculate
and write; but when he finishes

a project, he puts it away,
    and speaks of it dismissively
forever. Twelve,

    I stood on his shoulders.
His hands clasped my ankles and
    we ran.

Another day
    closer to death:
one of his little sayings. And,

    upon nearing home
after a long drive, looks
    like the house is still standing.

## Inukshuk

She should be less wild,
seen as she is through bars, and placid.
At breast and haunch, her hide
a starry constellation
punched into tin. She would taste like water
dripping in the cistern, this rhinoceros,
iron in the water, truth, potatoes
in the cold cellar, residue
from a dental filling. I drifted off

last night and seemed
to be laying stones in a wall. The stones
spoke to one another with different
voices, but they were all me. One
my stomach, one my head, yet
only stones. The stone that is my knee
has given way, I hear it creaking.
The stone that is my head
is weeping. There's a cleft

runs down her back,
where the armour comes round
to meet itself. Her baby, her own
miniature, nudges between hind legs, urgent
to suckle what moisture
seeps from a cairn. But truth:
                                        she isn't brittle, she
will not crack. She sighs
and her sides expand.

# The caught-between, as children

A flat pebble
   skipped between one tropical country
and another:
        the stifled
apartment of my grandparents
where the television
speaks loudest, where fading
people love me, and the villa
   beside the mango tree. To get there
we drive through the legs
of the monkey god. I'm greeted
with a gift: an ape who chomps
at the bit. The house chitters,
crows, slithers. Kids
are adaptable;
         we keep secrets well. Why
upset our mothers, who have chosen
only words that brace, notions
to turn us
great good men?    Harry Belafonte
for instance, handsomest
guy on the planet.
        So I don't tell
when it strikes
that the origin
stories are god
   forsaken    or how
a magazine fell
open to the ghostly skin
   of a man who had tried
to burn off the black.

*Two*

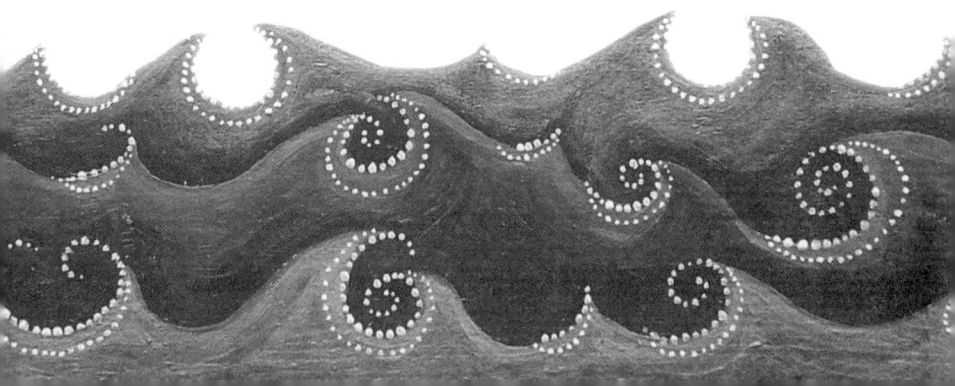

*You walk into the dance*


     ever so slightly off time, a snap
of the fingers and you're
the song. Your careless kick
teaches math to the dull-witted. It's a small
foot leads the body—narrow shoulders, ribs
like a boy, too-high waist, looming
head like the Wizard of Oz, empty
pockets, joints
so loose you might
all-of-a-moment collapse, ugly little
balsa wood man on a stick.

                                 Oh, but when
you move
         Gene Kelly turns too full
too smooth, white-toothed, altogether
congruous. Pity the man
with no toad-like charm; for it's you
who traces sublimity.
                   Imaginary
Paris: you in your top hat, line
of shadowy men in tails. Think
we know the drill. Casual
as ever, you aim your cane
and—pop. Pop. You're popping them
in the chest; they stagger, clutch,
fall. Rat-a-tat-
               a-tat-tat-tat, all
gunned down. There's
terror in it.

Like a catch in one's throat, your
almost imperceptible delays. With them
you give the dance a tongue —
                              as though
you're here, tugging at my sleeve. And just
before the curtain falls, your callous wave.

# The disintegration, as children

You would have thought,
what a gorgeous kid. You'd
have thought, what a sweetheart.
Gifted, gifted, they all said it.
I had an eye for colour, though now
I don't care. I let things be
what they are. What the hell
are we talking about? Oh,

my tragedies. Well, the big drama
was the children's train
but I was only two, so I hardly
knew the score. We made it just
under the wire. I guess
you could call us lucky. Grandma
and the rest of them gassed,
gone. Is that
how you like your luck?

I *was* loved, at least,
by my father. It was
a bit intense. My mother
was a manic stunner, depressive
eyeful. She was here and far.
They said

I had a kick in me
like a chorus line.
I cried in terror every night, clutched
the bed rail. And that
was long
before the coronary
to crown them all, before
my mother tipped
off the roof.
Before the tumours
came to roost. Tell me
it's a surprise
I have little faith in beauty.

*Messengers*


The bits of soap on the cardboard box smelled nice so I went back
I was bereft so I went the two blocks back
                                          to you whittling
pieces of Ivory                 face up Tourette's quick
and down                 this is the angel Gabriel you said
this is the angel Michael this is the angel so-and-so           I
learned from books you know Gothic Renaissance Romanesque
you know    and from my visions of course
                                    they don't really talk
no                              the angels don't judge they come
to find things out          then they go do you want a wolf
a lion
             bear?                              I intend
                                          to keep my bear
                                  close and secret through
                                    the evening swaddled
                                          in his soap wrapper
                                                though
neither secrets nor intentions
seem ever to stick                    and now dear god I'm
crying
in the bathroom of the restaurant before I've even had a drink the
paper won't come off the roll except in the smallest pieces
                                                and now
       standing at the bar beside my friend I place the bear on hind legs
                   all affection tell about the bear betray the bear
       my friend                                says he's heard

                                        memory's a groove
                        each time you return you only harm it
the more greatly it alters              from what it once was
he
reads me Borges' description
about coming upon two translations
of a Chinese philosopher's adage
more bewilderingly different interpretations
a person could not dream

                                                my friend

says he'd cooked this really delicious
asparagus
the other night
impressing his roommate        who proceeded to find for him
Proust's passages about asparagus remembered
                        my friend said   here were the two
asparaguses
(and he held out both hands as though to weigh)
and the written asparagus was so much
better
                                the bricks in the wall look like
                        books I say        my salad tastes good
                this Manhattan's too sweet
                                damn my heart I don't say
                        that your tongue can't tease it open.

## The face of Jennifer Lopez

I know I know
but in spite of all that
        a call runs through
my brain or blood
        that's mine I've lived there
or could
        this isn't the first time I've fallen
for an ignoble lady
        with a noble countenance
and still I'd vow
        like some hapless Mr. Bovary
here is a purity
        no crassness can belie
chin snug as a kayak
        dark wet eyes such
distances lie between
        our facial geometries
no slide flip or turn
        would align the planes
some see futility
        in the comparing of two fruits
but common
        sense glances off compulsion—
the weight of an apple
        is its substance
and its downfall
        and so it is with me
my dear

this gaze of mine
unravels its own agency
suicidal
as a rubber-shod pencil
the means to its own
erasure drowning
as they say
in your eyes I'm become
an unlikelihood
or at most a dull
and sexless child who knows
like the inside of its own mouth
the patterns in which
your animal hairs grow.
Perhaps it ought
to be acknowledged
you resemble my sister
my younger by three
years who is nut-
brown pale and rose-coloured all at once
who with violence
veers from the expected
to the instinctive
and back again
like a gymkhana barrel-
racer under the whip
some people find her difficult
others want her
at their parties
I have read my sister's
face for the floating
holiness she carries
I have read
her body also

foreign as an object
familiar as a familiar
    known
as though grafted onto my own
    a pear tree twisting
from my sturdy
    slivered side.

## Two sisters

Angelina was skinny; so frail and narrow,
one barely saw her as she stood
in the breezeway. If one could,
one saw two wrists, like sparrows,
fluttering to the ground; a sorry brace
for a farthing. But our father kept them from harm,
patiently fastening them back to her arms.
Eyes were the only feature of her face.

*How ugly,* I cried, and *Have some more dinner.*
*Hush Enza, I'm eating,* she'd whisper; moody,
lost, awash in her innards,
painfully gnawing morsels of fruit. She
watched in despair as her body grew thinner
while I feasted my way to beauty.

# Touring the mines at sundown

1.
Glittering mouths
in the rock beneath our feet, crystalline
openings above our heads.

Chunk of amethyst, weighing
460 kilos. Three months, a lone miner would take
to chisel it from the rock;

although, as we can see, this stone's too pale
to be of any value. It's kept
to illustrate a point.


2.
We're all intensity
in the gift shop, bedecking ourselves
like bible-time harlots.

Why do women like to always
be buying things? a friend once asked, as I paid
for my toothpick holder at the Austin airport.

I gave him a look.
But I do not use toothpicks.
In the guarded vault

the young bronzed couple,
boyish and tense, respectively,
are choosing a ring.

A whisper
among the husbandless: this blue bracelet
has stained my wrist blue.

The trinket returns to its tray.
Time. The bus
wants to take us to our hotel. It's dark,

the hills
have emptied. Now,
we tell one another, that was worth seeing.

## Lotus

Woodcut of a sitting lady
whose thoughts are inside
woodcut clouds.

Lady with an achy back,
lady with a bouncing cheque.
Bounce, bounce.

It's okay to be bad
at breathing,
to wish the lampshade had no seam.

Okay to be a lousy mountain;
to think mountains are mountains
and you are not one.

Lady in toile de Jouy
bobbles on her bony bum.
Toile frustration.

Descending the ladder
a knee offers soft landing.
A sledgehammer falls.

Lady on the Blue Willow plate
spits nails.
Red as a beet.

Hush, little baby.
This I learned from the monks.
Anger is my little one.

At the bottom of the sea,
Blue Willow lady
tends to her baby.

Bubbles rise
till they gently flatten
into the ceiling of the sea.

A bubble says I'm bored.
A bubble says
I'm not bored anymore.

A bubble says this is nice.
A bubble says—
false alarm.

This bubble tugs.
Lady levitates above the sea floor.
Bubble yanks hard.

There she goes.
She's a gingerbread man!
Her mouth an o.

Up,
clutching her balloon.
A bubble says that's funny.

Everything's funnier
down here.
That's why the monks like it.

## The one-two punch, as children

I rode a seesaw
between screeching boredom
—obvious to all—and perfect giddiness
which I ably contained. Quite the one-two
punch. Life of the party,
I was. My recurring tuberculosis
appeared symptomless to me; only the doctor
could give a diagnosis. What was the point?
So it was with these vinegar
and gin emotions, manifesting
no difference to the untrained eye;
and I was my only professional.
                              Once,
playing on a construction site,
I could find no foothold to boost myself
out of the foundation hole.
The other children peered down,
mocked me, trapped like a mole,
heavy-lidded, left-handed, plain
as the nose on my face; as yet unformed
into that elegant whippet
I've met in later photos. Neither
myself. My mother
whisked me out and home, where
my spoon found the flaw
in the porcelain bowl of milk again
and again, and each time I wondered:
is it a little patch of sugar?

# Populations

*She is a system of mass and energy, she is pullulating*
*with cells growing and dying, she is a motif in a Dutch*
*painting...*

—A.S. Byatt, *Still Life*

Ideas come quick
and cold. You do not spare us
your allusions, wield details
like a march of flags (pale mackerel
skies; the fat mauve flesh of a woman,
both like and unlike asters, cyclamen;
dark glitter of hanging honey-pot
ants whose distensible bellies, poured full
with nectar, feed a colony. Babies' heads,
which smell of biscuits.
                              Only you
would think it halfway sane to write a novel
that plunges
down every shrinking corridor
lest you miss the chance to discuss, say,
the sound of "diurnal" in a line of poetry), words
about words.
                    *All things to all men,*
you quote as you quote
all that's worthy. Greedy, compelled
to envelop; your slips inside reflection
followed always by an easy withdrawal. Even
knowledge of said greed, elucidated.

Elucidate this, word lady—
except I'm learning
the lay of the land.
No bombshells, but it seems
you've implanted some weird
appetite for seeing
from every earthly angle.
                              Then
you suck the breath from me and breathe it hot
into another's mouth. The paper
has a pulse. It shouldn't be possible.
Like a list (and you talk about lists) of organs
(and you talk about organs) that goes on
and on, past tedium,
past nausea. The teeth
suddenly grab, the gears turn, a dark
locomotive bears down the track. Is this
how it works: simply by naming, naming
to death? A fast refusal to let anything slide
unspoken? How is it that I understand
to point of desperation the intricate
yearnings of every alien brain
that populates your wondrous
ugly head? But I do.

*Dog with a rat*


      I'd tunnel
to that mythic time
      when the word was the thing
and beauty meant good
      to touch; naturally
bound
      and gagged
I'd do less damage
      or perhaps
if you
      hit me across the mouth
the suggestion smacks of sex
      when I'm wanting only
discipline
      though who's to believe me
words are nimble they
      do their own work and
we're lazy masters
      in the end
it's the greed that's striking
      to hate the sound
of one's own voice and still
      gobble up air as though
it were fifty boiled eggs
      why
just the other night
      a woman on the bus
holding her hot dog aloft
      berated a very drunken stranger

who'd said swallow bitch
    more distinctly
than he'd intended
    who could blame her
you're thinking; but she chased him
    around the bus saying
I'm gonna beat the crap out of you
    towering over him as he flinched
and shook and
    I'll kill you swear to God;
until sitting down heavily at last
    she said with wonder
can't remember the last time
    I had so much fun.

# Pockets full of chocolate, as children

Already true as turnips. Arguing with the brilliant young conservatives against slavery, all sense and morality on your side, you were creamed nonetheless. Never mind, Lord Hugh said kindly; we're not half as earnest as you think.

The mist began to clear. You turned witty, self-deprecating, cocksure, each in perfect measure. Fending off the Great Shaggy Bears, as you called the Boers with fondness, you were grazed by bullets that never found their mark.

Prisoner of war, you bolted—jumped trains, waded swamps, pockets full of chocolate. In enemy country, you rapped on a random door; it was answered by the only Englishman for miles. He drew the drapes and fed you leftover mutton.

Three days you slummed in a mineshaft, white rats galloping across your chest as you slept. Rather nice little beasts. And you'd been given a roasted chicken, after all, some books and candles, a bottle of scotch and a box of cigars.

You burrowed inside a mound of wool in the back of a truck. Stuffed in there for sixteen hours with some meat and a melon, you crossed the border. Emerging, you shot your revolver into the air with joy.

I'm half in love with you. Never mind that you grew ugly so young; by thirty, your pompous good looks subsumed by froggish complacency. There hangs at Pickwick's Choice a painted portrait you'd despised. Yet it holds you more than any photo.

Old man, you play me like a violin. You wished that your father had been a shopkeeper, and you his assistant, so you might have known him.

*Measured*

We pace the clear-shorn paths
of the labyrinth; steer
sharp turns, dizzy ourselves
in Fibonacci spirals. Sniff roses,
much too open. You loosen
your neckerchief as I idly
twirl my parasol. Perched
upon a well-placed boulder,
watch a Japanese family spread a picnic. Women
have flattered my shoulders, but never you. Do you think
the rhyme cheap? It's a train
of thought, that's all; forget it.
Sailboats in the distance, like
laundry on a clothesline. The lake
is calm; domestic, you would say, if
the lake were a poem. Sun bouncing
on the surface, thousands of tiny waves.
It would take an age to reproduce
such scenery with paper tole.

Just beneath, something speckled, swift, pale-bellied, long
glides parallel to shore. Cold, gentle submarine.

False to imply this fish has more reality than we,
disingenuous. But I'm tempted.

# Seven seasons: An omnibus

The detective has a fever; the train car glows red. In the barely
moving air, a sour smell rises from his pants. Hours ago, he'd
spilled his coffee while the elderly Polish couple across from him
continued to eat their sandwiches in heavy silence. Through half
closed eyes, he watches flaming silos and blistering hay-bales
as they pass. The body was hanging in a barn. He takes another sip
of water: glass heavy in his hand, the water tepid.

In the darkly gleaming foyer, whiffs of pot roast soaked in
wine. Spoons and glasses clink through the open door; amiable
rumble of a professor holding forth, snatches of laughter. The
body was stabbed repeatedly. The detective's eye is caught by the
intricate stained glass lancet at the top of the stairs, solemnly
depicting a lamb with halo and staff. It casts a bright mosaic
on the marble floor.

This pea soup, thick and full of pink, yielding shreds of ham, is
fortifying. Polyester roses, vinyl tablecloths: he's ducked in here
for some relief from the relentless drizzle. Through the cheap
Venetian blinds, a fine film of dust on each slat, he keeps half
an eye on the mud-spattered pickup. The body had been shot
at close range. A slight pulsing in his forehead; he registers the
hum of the fluorescent bulbs, spoons another bit of salted ham.

Beneath the silver maples of the old courthouse, children roll their Easter eggs. Little girls with smocked dresses in candy colours; boys wearing implausibly white shirts; their mothers shod in fashionable pumps that leave divots in the moist soil. The body was poisoned. The detective accepts a dainty from Mariano's wife, whose eyes are lush and dark against her creamy skin. Lemonade punch fizzes in his mouth.

On a white expanse of frozen lake, he stands before the ramshackle ice-fishing hut. Feeling a bit foolish, he knocks. The old man ushers him into a haze of tobacco smoke, sucking noisily on his pipe. Bone-numbing frigidity; the detective takes curious satisfaction in the ebb and flow of his crystallizing nose hairs. The body was found near to shore, trapped under the ice. The fishing line stretches, motionless.

It's lovely, this fog, warm and milky. Yellow slickers shuffle in and out of the mist, moving gradually around the pond's perimeter. Constables pulling the dredge. Muffled searchlights glide and bob. There is no body. He thinks of the boy's mother and father waiting in the farmhouse kitchen; gentle tick of the Delft clock, steam as it rises from a kettle. Dull black bible on the table, soft as an invertebrate.

A loud crack. The detective finds himself startled awake in the library, surrounded by precarious stacks of files; outside, a thunderstorm thrashes the trees. The night librarian has kindly dimmed the lights. He wipes a string of saliva from his mouth, stiffly bends down to unlace his shoes. His feet throb. The body knows when it's time to retire. Lately, he's been feeling the weather.

## The divine, as children

He comes at night
soft as sneakers.

The lights from passing traffic
thud across our ceilings,

water glasses, scotch
and water, mugs of tea gone cold.

He picks us up, each
in turn, like parsnips

he's found soaking in the sink.
Smoothes his thumb across

the latticed outskirts
of our eyes

trails his fingers through our hairs
of which he knows the number

but doesn't care. He's incidentally
autistic. As a boy

the mathematician Paul Erdos
would ask his mothers' friends

their birthdays; in exchange
he'd name the number of seconds

they'd been alive. A party trick
not the essential thing—

but an aspect thereof. Speed,
knowledge, tickle our dim wits;

*we just want to be held.*
He grasps our bruised fat as though

what could be better? Rubs the length
of our bones, he's teasing

out the arthritis oh          god
presses the sweet spot

and sighing in his open hands
we leak. He has no wish

to pare away this body, bring
to light some reed-like soul.

Nothing repels. Stickiness is
something to dip a finger in.

*Three*

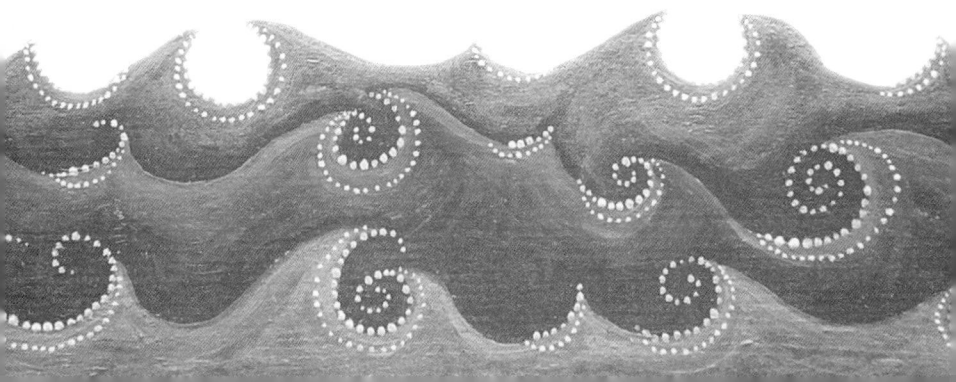

## The disintegration, as wraith

1.
You chalk me up ethereal. I didn't ask
for this story.
                    Those brittle vessels
I collected? They're mourning, sure,
anyone can see it. They nod to one another, bow
ever so slightly at the waist; turned
face, bent ear.
                    Give 'em a minute.
All befuddled dignity
at a singles' event. They're a bit
old for this sort of thing.
                    Wait,
did you catch that? Those two,
out and out flirting! She thrusts
her hip, he leans in. They murmur:
what about the ropes?
        what about the wires?


2.
What about the mounds of balls?
No more clues; I've given
everything you need. You guys
would write an obituary
for a wadded-up serviette.

3.
The latex weeps
on the gallery floor.
You're hanging
my stuff all wrong
in last-ditch efforts.

You quibble: another tragedy
versus an apt eventuality. Either way,
it was the only outcome. The sheets,
they're out of my hands.
If I gave the world a hiccup,
good for me. At this point
I take what I can get.

4.
Without my tools
or materials, I've learned to kill
time. When I'm sick
of the river, I haunt the airport.

I still know what I'm doing.

## On the death of another world

Tall and gentle, smudgy-eyed,
none of us doubted you, ever.
You fell in love, grew lean,
earned your badge.
All about us, good men
became scoundrels
and perfectly lovely girls turned Jezebels
overnight; still, we knew
you were incorruptible.

Ryan, Ryan, your name,
that little loop—leap up,
my heart, fall
down.

It's still so hard to fathom.
Shot through the back
on the tracks by the river;
like that, so quick and brutal.
Your brother the mayor
seemed torn up enough.
Still we wonder.

We prayed you'd pull through—
were convinced, in fact,
that you'd be fine next week.
But your lips came quiet, and your skin
came cold. And they scooped out
those deep, smoky eyes of yours,

put them in a blind man
like currants in a cookie.

Bittersweet, these past few months,
to see that cowboy
winning the heart of your wife,
your eyes so tender
above his lush moustache.

## The shapeshifter, as children

A fifteen-year-old runaway. Also,
at times, a kidnapped boy,
victim of a savage

family, walk-away from a fiery smash-up
that turned my doting mum
to ash. Bandages swathed my head

or I was mute. Trauma
calmed me. I felt myself
shrink, bones unfuse.

Fourteen, French, sixteen,
Spanish. I called the shelters
trembling

as my pores closed tight, cheeks
a nectarine; swallowed
in a sweater

that knitted,
purled continually longer.
They'd find me curled

in a telephone booth, worm
of potential. Eyes welled
for me

and I'd been so thirsty.
Still I sprang
from any gesture, head down

until trust
screwed itself into place.
I moonwalked

among the humans. The other children
grew to love me, I helped them
with their homework.

Eyes glimmered when they saw me
thrive, steady
held me. I tell you this,

it never
was an act.
The authorities would begin to question

and I was trapped
where I'd started: healthy,
adult, singular.

## Stone lions

Look alive, dear friend. Our golden dish
has rolled away, yet the hour's lit with a light that's gone.

The bridge, the smelter by the lake, your
paw; each arcs, lengthens,

longs. See over there? That stump of a steeple
used to pierce the sky. Fierce she was, and gothic; but shocked

too easily. Storm after storm, lightning bore down
like paddles on a heart. Cut her down to size, they said.

Now we wend along the mountain's shaggy
side, watch the sheen of glass apartments

stutter with dusk. We haven't much time left.
Hamilton stinks of sulphur, or so they say; all

empty storefronts, layers of grime, tires
catching fire. Well, they don't like Buffalo either, or anything

monolithic. They like Vancouver, to be specific. Quit
flicking your tail at me—

oh. Have I used up the hour with words
again?

Your silence says Silence
but we know it doesn't suit me.

Our fur has lost its halo. At road's end,
the dim marble of a bird bath beckons;

we pad upon dark grass, loam, patio stone. Past the perfect
stillness of the hedgerows. Shadows move upon the sheers. We

slink back
to our pedestals, and jump up.

## Thirty

Judas, you have such beautiful eyes, the shape of commas in your sorrow. For that, they don't hate you any less.

Through the offbeat gaze of Lloyd Webber, you've got the good of the people at heart. One self-righteous Afro-Judean calling the pot black. But young! Fair busting with passion. He had you singing, glorious.

The way I see it, you made no choice. You drank a jug or two of wine; some pretty girl or boy unfolded a silver palm; and this you came to want. Such hungers are no mystery. Tracing bounty with the tip of a finger, christened yourself a traitor. Your grave failing, inertia.

Approaching him in the garden, you didn't think to love him. When the guards bound his arms, you'd already begun to forget. But your heart was in the kiss.

## Thumbnail Venus

Why should songs she sings and where
she dwells, the stuff she's of, diminish
me? As though she's the finished
piece and I the shavings on the floor.
The trick's to round me up again, back to square
one. I have some shape, I think. My life is rich
in ways a), b), and c), and while I wish
for something more,
her sharing of your morning paper is irrelevant,
I tell myself, myself I tell,
the words bounce back and forth but make no dent
within my tinny walls. But well
I give, well I receive; me and mine, haven't we spent
some pleasant moments waiting coyly on the half-shell?

## Sunday

Ruddy cheeks, long lashes, tongue
like a boy. I'm filling up
like a glass of milk,

tuning fork, vaulted
ceiling. A hand on my shoulder
where there is no hand.

I look down at your shoes.
They say, *husband.*
And so you are.

## Statement of faith

My friend makes a living
by replicating sounds for moving pictures: Chevy
hits the guardrail, white stallion
gallops across the sand.

Someone else crosses the genes of a tomato
with those of a fish.

To his live studio audience,
the psychic says, *I'm hearing from someone*
*who died in the woods. Someone whose name*
*begins with an M.*

Fire, wheel, coin,
gunpowder, tinned kippers. In lesser news, a man
leaps to catch a football;

his wife, mouthful of pins,
takes in the sleeve
on her dressmaker's mannequin.
An egg is weighed.

*Marlene? Martine?* Is this man a charlatan
or does he speak with ghosts? More than once,
the spirits who come
have been relations of the second cameraman
who is shy.

Some people think
we're infinitely
negligible. Apartment blocks,
square upon square;

frying up onions, thumbing
through dirty magazines.

The psychic has trouble convincing him
to set the camera down.

## The inelegant equestrian, as children

Once, a plane fell out of the sky
as I watched through the nursery window.
At five, I had a nightmare: the massive wave,
the great ship sinking, the blurred
man. That night
the *Titanic* went down.
                              I blame myself.
More prolonged disasters
followed. Years confined at boarding school,
damp with the smell of farts.
My loins thumped; my mind
was sandwiched in cellophane. Look,
grown-ups pointed, at the night sky
or the emerald river or gold-dappled hills.
                                          No.
Alone in the darkroom, I drank hypo;
downed bottles of hay fever drops; swallowed
20 aspirin at a trick. A lousy horseman,
I took stupid jumps on the Common,
fed myself deadly
nightshade. With a dull penknife,
I tried to saw my knee open.
                              I couldn't
abide the monotony. I lay in a field,
twirling the chambers. I lived.
I lived. I lived. A bullet of adrenaline,
help me bear the dull thud of time.

## Tenor

Mottled thighs are marble
underwater. Our thin white hairs float

like scratches on a cornea.
The sun

shafts from the skylight
through to the blue floor, flicker

on a film reel.
We are whales,

fat and taut, heavy
with days.

It's humid. We paddle so slowly,
patient as flies in amber. Close

to soundless space: the staggered beating
light dark light, a human sigh, static of breathing,

except those days he comes, holding
his white head above water. We thought

it was another language he sang, I
would have sworn it was opera.

The sorrow in this pool
is like mercury. It rolls without warning.

## Public radio

Car heater's on full blast. Jeans soaked through, my skin's clam-cold. The storm hit just as we packed up our tools for the day. We waited it out in the shack, slouching in the smoke with our drinks; dirty, cracking bad jokes, surrounded by half-naked pinups.

Monica from Mexico asks the DJ how high the moon; it's her grandma's birthday. I'll be home soon. A transport truck quakes by, sluices puddles at my windshield. Everything grey except that sleek white Lincoln and did anyone ever sing her heart out like this? Crying just a little, maybe I'm sensitive from the caesar—limes and celery, the guys went all out today.

Now a British gentleman reads Carol Shields. *I like Tallis precisely because he is second-best, she said. I don't expect you to understand. I do, I do! he cried in his awful voice.*

They were talking about the sizes of their trowels. Mine's eleven inches—much easier on the hand. Dead serious.

## Crimson

I've compared white paint chips under various lights:
ivories, bones, the whites with pinkish undertones;
off-whites that read white. Snow White.
True White. Whiter than.
                  My two-year-old
evolves long-term plans
to ripen into Cinderella
as I bring her juice,
scrub the tub, go diving for oyster
nail polish in bins,
              99 cents,
                just the shade
          for half-pint fingers.    My lungs
pool red as she drills
for silver and gold as well    she drills    but I don't flee
or call for the woodcutter. This
is the job.
        I long
for an island
in the kitchen, regularly take
the car to travel three blocks. Under the bus
goes the Walmart boycott—
                we need
to baptize the baby
  in the waterfall
    of a white noise machine.
                It's me
that wants a dunking. In the darkening
cream of the baby's room, he looks

like my father's mother
and my mother-in-law's brother: elf
to dinner roll
and back again. This one? Flip.
Or that. Mine? Or not.
    If mine, how much? How long?
                              I pray
we're doing right by you. Heck,

this town is white. White son,
white daughter, would you believe

we were bohemians? Time
will tell.
       I nurse every
other hour, rock this salt
body, don't
die, don't die.          Morning's
early. The light, the sheet
covering my head.
                Gone the tender
                    dark, but there's a well
                      of a different colour.
I go to face them.
Diaper, milk,
bra, bread,
knuckles—

however they shriek
I can drown them out.

## The mirthless, as children

A small girl in sooty Allegheny
I wore a veil
to shield my face from coal dust.
We all did this.
The doctor's daughter, I was not
to be kissed by adults
and I did not permit it. I knew my body.
I extended my hand.
Obscured by lace that bleak city was
almost alluring.
Only liars called me
pretty. After
William died at one, I was the son
my parents fleeting had.
Willful—that will not surprise any—
and throbbing
to ancient myths my father told at bed.
I wanted to hold
the baby Achilles and dip him wholly.
Is the water pure?
Father once asked me of droplets
on a slide. Yes.
Are you certain, Martha?
I was sure.
He placed my eye against
the microscope;
I was young enough that I stood
upon a pile of books.
I peered in the lens and was disturbed, and cried:

But there are wriggles!
I saw the ugly side of truth, have seen
it ever since.

Mother and Father believed I was one thing;
they were my audience.
As I ironed the handkerchiefs to perfection,
I could feel the unknown
quantity of my soul!—the viscera
bristling, the shifting
weight of the lion as he paces,
the yearn of my heel.

## In the bedroom

Three leaves, each bigger than my hand, have been on the night table for over a year. Once green and lusty, then streaked with yellow like toads from the jungle, they now are dry and colourless; you can snap them like pappadum. If the leaves were ears, they would have heard the humans happening. Clasping of hooks and eyes; clearings of phlegm and snot; a confession. We, who cannot split a carton of fries with ease, might be sharing everything.

But then, the bedroom is undulating with aliveness—every surface bristles in its microscopic way. The dresser's edge is not so sharp as it goddamn feels; thigh's flesh and oak yield one to the other. Breath, voice, filaments of hair are plumbed by the inhabitants of our beds, colonists of our skin.

Also. The black swirling emptiness my sister's husband saw, through cover of dark, in the upper left corner of their room. He stared at it terrified and didn't want to wake her. After a while he heard her small voice: do you feel it too?

## Loose connections, as children

Stained mattresses sprawled
across the Las Vegas desert.

Dead hawks lay
thick on our roof.

Mom placidly pieced
her Norman Rockwell

puzzles. Before I could grasp
a paddle was taped

to my hand; days spent swatting
my custom-crafted mobile

of tennis balls. Good times, I think,
infancy—and still, at three,

with my sawed-off racket.
Salt-shakers flew. I thought

I was something.
*Stop thinking!*

Pops paced, rifle in hand.
The balls rained down. Dear me

what's left of you?
Dangly earrings, wad

of whisky-soaked tobacco.
After a while, I looked

out into the crowd
to see myself everywhere,

jean shorts and frosted mullets.
A bundle of loose connections,

who could tell? Once
in a while, wires touched,

a spark. Not much,
just enough. When the preacher told me God

wasn't Pops, I made him say it
three times over.

A teaspoon of hope
for me,

a distant shape
growing closer. Here I came.

# Notes

Earlier versions of some of these poems have appeared in *Arc, The Fiddlehead, Prairie Fire* and *The Montreal Prize Longlist Anthology.*

The E. Nesbit epigraph can be found in her memoir *Long Ago When I Was Young* (London: Ronald Whiting and Wheaton Ltd., 1966).

The Winston Churchill epigraph is taken from a speech made to the Canadian Parliament in 1941, as printed in *The Unrelenting Struggle: War Speeches by the Right Hon. Winston Churchill C.H., M.P.,* compiled by Charles Eade (Boston: Little, Brown & Company, 1942).

The "As children" poems wouldn't exist without the following autobiographies, diaries, interviews and articles. Because, as a reader, I'd want to know, I've also clearly identified those who inspired these poems:

p. 12 Susan Sontag ("The ferocious list-maker"). Sources included Susan Sontag's *Reborn: Journals and Notebooks, 1947–1963,* edited by David Rieff (New York: Farrar, Straus & Giroux, 2008) and Eleanor Wachtel's *Original Minds: Conversations with CBC Radio's Eleanor Wachtel* (Toronto: Harper Perennial, 2003).

p. 18 Daniel Tammet ("The kaleidoscope"). Sources included Daniel Tammet's *Born on a Blue Day* (London: Hodder & Stoughton, 2006) and a radio interview with Tammet conducted by Anne Strainchamps (aired by *To the Best of Our Knowledge,* February 11, 2007; produced by Wisconsin Public Radio).

p. 23 Jackie Chan ("The fearless hyena"). Sources included *I Am Jackie Chan: My Life in Action* (New York: Ballantine, 1998).

p. 31 Barack Obama ("The caught-between"). Sources included Barack Obama's *Dreams from My Father* (New York: Times Books, 1995).

p. 37 Eva Hesse ("The disintegration"). Sources included Cindy Nemser's *Art Talk: Conversations with 12 Woman Artists* (New York: Scribner, 1975) and Vanessa Corby's *Eva Hesse: Longing, belonging and displacement* (London: I.B. Tauris, 2010), Lucy Lippard's *Eva Hesse* (New York: New York University Press, 1976).

p. 49   Roland Barthes ("The one-two punch"). Sources included Roland Barthes' *Roland Barthes* (New York: Farrar, Straus & Giroux, 1977).

p. 54   Winston Churchill ("Pockets full of chocolate"). Sources included Winston Churchill's *My Early Life: A Roving Commission* (London: Thornton Butterworth, 1930).

p. 69   Frédéric Bourdin ("The shapeshifter"). Sources included David Grann's *The Chameleon: The Many Lives of Frédéric Bourdin* (The New Yorker, August 11, 2008) and Mick Brown's *The Imposter: Interview with the Chameleon* (*The Telegraph*, August 11, 2012).

p. 78   Graham Greene ("The inelegant equestrian"). Sources included Graham Greene's *Fragments of Autobiography* (London: Penguin, 1991).

p. 83   Martha Graham ("The mirthless"). Sources included Martha Graham's *Blood Memory* (New York: Doubleday, 1991).

p. 86   Andre Agassi ("Loose connections"). Sources included Andre Agassi's *Open* (New York: Knopf Doubleday, 2009).

The poem "Populations" owes an obvious debt to A.S. Byatt's *Still Life* (New York: Simon & Schuster, 1985).

The poem "Public radio" includes lines from Carol Shields' short story "New Music" from *Dressing Up for the Carnival* (Toronto: Random House, 2000).

I'm forever grateful to the Imperial gang in all its configurations: Adam Dickinson, Jessica Johnson, David Seymour, Charmaine Tierney, Matthew Tierney and Andy Weaver. Particular and heartfelt thanks to Katia Grubisic and Steve McOrmond. You gave what I needed.

This book is for Jamie, with love and wonder.

Adrienne Barrett's poems have been published in *Arc*, *Prairie Fire* and *The Fiddlehead*. Her long poem, "Madonna with three childless writers," was longlisted for the 2011 Montreal Prize. *The house is still standing* is her first collection. She lives in Woodstock, Ontario.